D0707469

Dyslexia
students
in
need

Dyslexia
students
in
need

PAT HEATON B.Ed. (Hons) M.Ed.
Royston Dyslexia Unit
and
Gina Mitchell B.A. (Hons), Ph.D.
University of Bradford

W

WHURR PUBLISHERS
LONDON AND PHILADELPHIA

© 2001 Whurr Publishers
First published 2001 by
Whurr Publishers Ltd
19b Compton Terrace, London N1 2UN, England and
325 Chestnut Street, Philadelphia PA 1906, USA

All rights reserved. No part of this publication may be
reproduced, stored in a retrieval system, or transmitted
in any form or by any means, electronic, mechanical,
photocopying, recording or otherwise, without the
prior permission of Whurr Publishers Limited.

This publication is sold subject to the conditions that it
shall not, by way of trade or otherwise, be lent, resold,
hired out, or otherwise circulated without the
publisher's prior consent in any form of binding or
cover other than that in which it is published and
without a similar condition including this condition
being imposed upon any subsequent purchaser.

British Library Cataloguing in Publication Data
A catalogue record for this book is available from the
British Library.

ISBN: 1 86156 179 2

Printed and bound in the UK by Athenaeum Press Ltd,
Gateshead, Tyne & Wear

Contents

Preface

It has been estimated that 10 per cent of the population are dyslexic, though many are thought to conceal their problems to avoid the stigma associated with the disability. However, despite this, evidence suggests that the number of dyslexic students entering Further and Higher education has increased significantly.

Currently, this category of disability numerically outstrips all others; it is further distinguished by its definition as a learning disability, which can create a crippling level of underachievement if appropriate support and remediation are not forthcoming.

In addition, a recent survey has indicated that 43 per cent of those with dyslexia in Further and Higher Education are identified only after embarking on their degree and higher-level studies.

The factors outlined above indicate that there exists an urgent need for accessible and practical advice not only for those with dyslexia but also for teaching and administrative staff in colleges and universities offering courses and places to a wide range of students.

How to use this book

Many students will benefit from starting with the Checklist and Screening and Assessment (Flow Chart) – see pages xxi and xxiii.

However, you may prefer to choose a particular chapter from the Contents, page vii.

About the authors

Pat Heaton has been screening and teaching dyslexics for more than 20 years. She is Director of Teaching at the Royston Dyslexia Unit and her published works include *Dealing with Dyslexia, Learning to Learn, Parents in Need,* and the *Pat's Cats* and *Pam and Tom* reading schemes.

Gina Mitchell works in the Disability Office at the University of Bradford and has responsibility for the screening, diagnosis and support of students and staff who have dyslexia. Her first contact with dyslexia occurred when her eldest child was found to be dyslexic at primary school. At that time, she was a mature student herself and she went on to work in higher education as a lecturer and examiner.

Acknowledgements

Our thanks are due to many people who have helped in the production of this book, particularly the students who completed and commented on the questionnaires, Peter Honey Publications and the British Dyslexia Association. Students with dyslexia and staff in the Disability Office at the University of Bradford offered unfailing help as well as constructive criticism. In addition, we are most grateful to Dr Mike Page and to 'Karen' and 'Tim' for providing us with case histories drawn from their own experience.

We must also thank our families and friends for their support, Lyndon's contribution being much appreciated and especially valuable.

Introduction

This book is for anyone interested in dyslexia. More particularly, it is for any adult student involved in Further or Higher Education who believes he or she is dyslexic, whether or not he or she has been formally assessed as being disabled by the syndrome.

That the term 'dyslexia' means difficulty with words or language is now fairly well known. It is also recognized that there may be other underlying deficits at all stages and ages.

Increasingly, younger 'phonologically disabled' children (dyslexics) are identified at primary school and taught by qualified specialists. However, the situation for adults is rather different.

As study-skills tutors working in Further and Higher Education, we are very aware of an 'expertise gap' at this level. Adult learning support services vary considerably. Some institutions provide excellent screening, assessing, counselling and teaching facilities; others are reported and observed to be less well organized.

Given these circumstances, we felt that students with dyslexia needed their own dyslexia-aware text, that they would benefit from knowing how other dyslexic students had coped with learning/returning and that they would welcome tutors' advice on their very special needs.

We have also observed that long, complicated texts often create more problems than they solve for people with reading/ordering problems. We know that most people with dyslexia dislike small print, crowded pages and 'unnecessary' detail.

Briefly then, that is the background to this book's style, content and aspirations. The text is – we hope – both dyslexia-centred and dyslexia-aware. We have tried to be both practical and realistic. For the reasons stated, we have focused on the basics and limited the number of topics and pages. Plain language and order have been a priority. All chapters, for instance, follow a similar pattern: students' responses to a questionnaire item are followed by suggestions for dealing with the particular difficulty, and every chapter ends with a summary.

Having already published a questionnaire-based text, we decided to use the same method of research. We tried to identify priorities and difficulties, and after listening to students with dyslexia, we decided on six basic questions – one for each chapter.

The first questionnaire was sent out in May 1997 and 14 students responded. Their comments informed the final design, which is reproduced on page xix. This second version was sent to 63 adult students; it was fully completed by 40 of them. A variety of courses and institutions was represented. Verbal feedback was also helpful.

All 40 students approved the checklist and the screening and assessment basic guide. At this stage, we also dicovered that coloured overlays placed over the text helped most of the students involved in our research. (For further information about coloured overlays see Appendix 17, page 91). When using this book, many students will benefit from starting with the checklist (p xxi) and the screening and assessment basic guide (p xxii). However, others may prefer to choose a particular chapter from the list of contents.

Finally, we take full responsibility for the research, questions and style, and thank the students for their advice and good wishes.

Pat Heaton
Gina Mitchell

The questionnaire

1   Which aspect of starting your course worried you most and why? (See Chapter 1)

2   Thinking of study skills, what is your biggest problem and why? (See Chapter 2)

3   Assuming your own experiences have been fairly typical, what advice would you give to other dyslexics who are thinking of studying for a degree? (See Chapter 3)

4   What resources, strategies and advisers have proved helpful in the day-to-day management of your course? (See Chapter 4)

5   Given that resources are limited, which one resource would you prioritize and why? (See Chapter 5)

6   In universities and colleges of further education, assessment is normally based on coursework as well as examinations. Which would you prefer and why? (See Chapter 6)

Checklist
Are you dyslexic?*

This checklist is used by the British Dyslexia Association. If you have not been assessed but think you are dyslexic, look at the list below.

Read the following, but answer yes only if the problem happens frequently.

1   I read very slowly and may have to reread several times before I understand.

2   I lose my place or miss out lines when I am reading.

3   When I write I confuse words that are similar.

4   I make many spelling mistakes.

5   Some days I spell better than others.

6   I cannot copy things down accurately.

7   I dread being given complicated instructions.

8   I get confused about dates and times.

9   I find it difficult to organize myself.

10   I confuse left and right.

*Adapted with permission from: *Dyslexia: Signposts to Success*. British Dyslexia Association, 98 London Road, Reading RG1 5AU.

11   Many of my difficulties get worse under stress.

12   I am often thought to be lazy.

13   I try to improve but feel frustrated by the above.

Most people will answer yes to a few of the points listed here. However, if you answer yes to eight or more you may well be dyslexic.

Now turn to Dyslexia: Screening and Assessment (a basic guide) on the next page.

Dyslexia: Screening and Assessment (a basic guide)

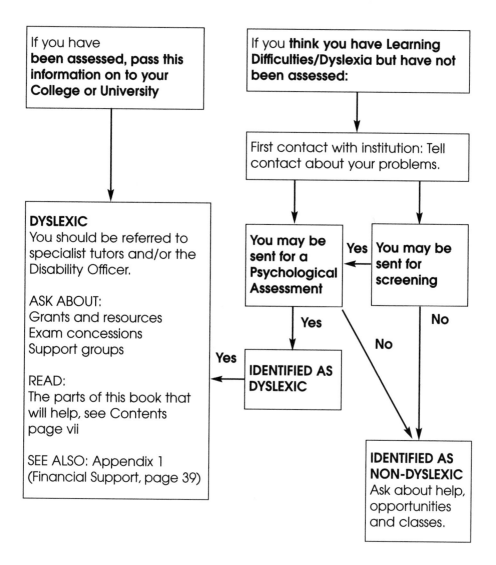

Note: For information on Schools of Health Studies see also Appendix 2, page 44.

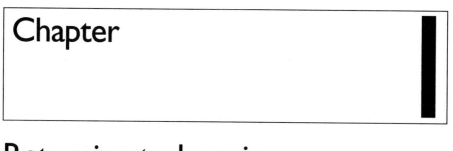

Chapter 1

Returning to learning

Fears and expectations

Reference: Questionnaire item 1: Which aspect of starting your course worried you most and why?

> Every student was concerned about more than one aspect of his or her course. Also, academic conventions worried the entire sample. A majority mentioned the workload.

The following comments about the volume of work are typical.

I was worried about all the reading and how I would manage to take it all in. I know I read slowly and sometimes I don't know what I have read 10 minutes later.

I was worried about the workload and keeping up. I've had problems in the past.

I was expecting an overbearing amount of work with little or no support structure. (This has proved to be wrong.)

I have to spend a lot of time reading over material twice in order to understand it, so that makes it hard. I don't find reading enjoyable but obviously it is required.

Not being able to keep up with the work and the lectures was a worry. I thought it might all be too fast for me.

I knew a large amount of work was involved and I knew what it was like to get behind. This bothered me but I also know how good it feels when you achieve despite your difficulties.

Academic/literary conventions and styles caused concern.

Because of dyslexia, there is a big divide between conceptual abilities and logical argument for essays. Also, it's hard to construct coherent arguments into words on paper and to put my own ideas into the right sort of language.

I was really worried about my grammar and style because I have been criticized in the past but I didn't know how to improve them.

I was worried about the style of writing for essays - I knew it had to be different from what I'd done in school but I didn't know how.

Referencing was a problem. It has been explained to me but I still get mixed up; I think it's something to do with the ordering. I've always had problems in that area and they don't get any better!

Moving on to individual problems, more than half of the students had fears about some aspect of the course content.

I wasn't sure if my maths was good enough. I've had problems with maths before and there was a lot of maths involved in the course I wanted.

I also struggled with the medical terminology, which seems impossible to pronounce, let alone spell!

I was very worried about using a computer. I had absolutely no experience and thought people would just think I was stupid, that is the usual perception of dyslexic people.

Bad/negative experiences affected hopes and expectations.

Despite reassurances, I doubted the amount of personal empathy and educational support from my supervisor.

I assumed I would be misunderstood because I always had been - even by my own family!

> I always tried at school but the teaching didn't seem to suit me. I never quite knew what they wanted and I didn't enjoy learning.

> I was very worried about fitting in with a new group of people. I've had some painful and humiliating experiences in the past.

> I expected ignorance from lecturers – that's what I've been used to.

> You know there will be enormous setbacks, the most worrying aspects are lack of self-discipline and lack of confidence.

> I was concerned about having to organize all the many forms and documents associated with starting the course. I was sure I'd get something wrong and end up in a mess.

Only one of the sample mentioned funding.

> I knew I needed a laptop computer and I wondered whether I could afford to buy one.

Finally, lack of confidence was mentioned or implied by every respondent, some of whom described their earlier educational experiences and 'failures' at length.

Suggestions

Do:

1   Ensure that anyone involved in your education/course understands dyslexia and its implications.

Try to see all your tutors individually. Carry copies of relevant leaflets from the British Dyslexia Association (BDA). These can be distributed as appropriate. The BDA's address is 98 London Road, Reading RG1 5AU (tel: 0118 966 2677). Their publications cover many different aspects of dyslexia. For example, *Information For Adult Dyslexics* is subject-centred, while *Recognising Dyslexia* gives general background information.

Do some preparation before you contact the BDA. If you phone, have details of your course and a list of your problems/questions to hand. Help the charity to help you.

2   Consider alternative ways of obtaining and recording information. Ask if you might tape-record lectures and/or make other special arrangements.

Some lecturers will hand out lecture notes, copies of visual aids and so forth before the lecture.

3   Take advantage of modern technology.

Word processors, spell checkers and some computer programs are excellent for dyslexics. (See References and Resources section on pages 93 to 96 for further details.)

4   Ask the Disability Officer about your rights, concessions and assessment procedures.

You may be entitled to a Disabled Students' Allowance (DSA), a scribe in examinations, and extra time. Validating bodies vary so you need to find out what's on offer.

5   Check out support groups for dyslexics.

If your institution doesn't have one, ask whether you might start one. Again, you might approach the Disability Officer and/or the Dyslexia Support Co-ordinator.

6   Be realistic about what you expect to achieve and the time it will take to achieve it.

You will probably have to put in extra time and energy to gain your qualification. You may, for instance, have to redraft an essay three or four times before achieving an 'average' grade.

7   Find out about all the learning support services.

Dyslexia support groups have already been mentioned. You might try a maths/English workshop. Some colleges and universities also offer extra study-skills sessions. Attend these if you're unsure about: **note-taking, referencing, bibliographies, styles of writing** and so forth.

This book combines formal and informal writing styles. The first part of each chapter is quite formal, the suggestions section much less so. See Appendices 3 to 7 on pages 45 to 53 for exercises and tips on **basic referencing, note-taking and formal writing**.

Unless told otherwise, use a formal style. It is easy to change personal to formal. For example:

- 'I feel' converts to 'it appears that/apparently'
- 'I think' converts to 'it seems that/seemingly'
- 'I believe' converts to 'it could be argued that/arguably'.

If all study skills are a problem, talk to the Disability Officer and/or ask the Librarian for suitable books. (See section on *Helpful books* on pages 94 and 95.)

8   Try to be highly organized. Lists often help. Make, keep and update them. Arrange your life so that you have time to read and reread, write and rewrite. You might have to sacrifice some social activities.

Photocopy important papers. Keep a diary and note (almost) anything and everything! Enter times and dates for tutorials. Get into the habit of noting the dates you submit assignments/post documents/make important telephone calls.

Organize lecture notes. They should always begin with highlighted titles and dates. Keep separate files for each subject and write titles on the back and front and top and bottom. Titles should be visible/legible whichever way the file is handled. If possible, use contrasting colours for different subjects.

Clear plastic wallets are useful for filing material that needs regular and/or further attention.

9   Make a positive effort to improve spelling. If it is really bad, you may need a remedial language programme such as Alpha to Omega. You would probably benefit from specialist tuition. Ask the Disability Officer about this.

Many dyslexics use a Franklin Spellchecker. Buy one if you dislike conventional dictionaries. Buy a small notebook to use as a personal dictionary and carry it around. Label the pages alphabetically and (carefully) enter the words you find difficult. Use spare moments to revise spellings/invent mnemonics. (See examples in Appendix 8 on page 54.)

10   Talk to your tutors if you feel you're falling behind and/or you are confused about something. Generally, tutors are more dyslexia-aware than they have ever been. Refer to the Dyslexia Support Tutor or Disability Officer if problems continue.

11   If you can't deliver what's required, your course and/or the teaching style may not suit you. Psychologists have analysed the way we learn into four types: Activist, Reflector, Theorist, Pragmatist. A simple test will help you to identify your style. (See examples of questions in Appendix 9 on page 57.)

North Yorkshire TEC publishes a free introduction to this subject, called *How do you do it?* (Freephone: 0800 515547).

Also, your Disability Office may have the test to hand. If not, it can be ordered from Peter Honey Publications, 10 Linden Avenue, Maidenhead, Berkshire SL6 6HB (tel: 01628 633 946; web site: www.peterhoney.co.uk).

12 Use Post-it notes liberally. If you think you'll forget things, stick a Post-it checklist where you're bound to spot it.

Post-its also make good bookmarks. Stick them down the sides of pages to which you'll want to return. Write a key word(s) on each Post-it. Experiment with position. Try to place Post-its so that you can see key words at a glance/when the book is closed.

Summary

- Have confidence in your own ability. If you've got this far, you must have potential.

- Take one day at a time and keep calm. Don't waste valuable energy on pointless anxiety.

- Make all the necessary contacts as soon as possible (Disability Officer, Dyslexia Support Group and so forth).

- Organize your time/diary/files and all other resources. This will pay dividends later.

Chapter 2

Study skills

Reference: Questionnaire item 2: Thinking of study skills, what is your biggest problem and why?

Sentence construction, structure and argument, essays, reading, libraries, concentration, exam revision, spelling and note-taking were all mentioned.

More than half the sample identified cause and effect.

My bad memory causes me to produce badly constructed sentences and also to have to read things several times.

Making notes in lectures is difficult. I can't keep up because of my poor spelling.

If your spelling and reading are poor, the library is not your favourite place.

As I do not apply normal logic to a task, the end result is unpredictable. The outcome can be incredibly bad or very good, rarely average.

My poor ordering skills affect so many things. Numbers are problematic and statistics are a nightmare. I also spend a considerable time writing and rewriting sentences.

As my short-term memory is not good I find recall difficult, even straight after taking notes.

My poor organizational skills are a problem. I jump from idea to idea. The reader thinks this person doesn't know what the argument of the essay is about.

Being dyslexic means that I find the structuring of answers very difficult. What is logical and obvious to me isn't to others. I find it very difficult to word answers correctly.

Several students expected poor results in exams.

I have always been poor at exams. I have to spend a lot more time studying than someone whose performance does not deteriorate under exam pressure. I have to work very hard just to get an average result.

I wish I knew a way of coping with exam nerves and revising techniques.

Once I am in an exam situation my memory will go blank and I shall run out of time. I've never yet finished an exam paper.

I've never really known where and how to start revising.

Other dyslexics will understand these comments. Many students have problems with higher-level study skills, and dyslexics more so.

Having said that, experience has proved that poor learning habits and performance can be improved.

Suggestions

Do:

1   Change/improve your note-taking style. Aim to think more and write less.

Often, the main idea/argument appears in the first sentence of a paragraph/lecture. Ask yourself: 'What is his/her point here?' Try to be precise. Push yourself to find the exact word(s). (This is not easy but these skills are essential and transferable.)

When possible, use your own language and not the writer's. This will help you make sense of/recall the idea.

Note ideas rather than complete sentences. Try using 'spider plans' or 'mind maps'. (See examples and exercise in Appendices 3, 4, 5 and 6 on pages 45 to 49.)

2   Think of structure and content as two sides of the same coin. (Many students think the former less important; good writers consider both.)

A well-constructed sentence/paragraph/essay conveys content from writer to reader. Poorly constructed work suggests a limited understanding of content.

3   Consider your essay in terms of an argument. Keep essay plans simple. Plan an introduction, development and conclusion. Remember that each sentence should carry the argument forward to its conclusion.

Use link words to carry meaning from one paragraph to the next. Make sure that you understand key words in essay titles. (See examples of link words and key words in Appendices 10 and 11 on pages 58 to 61.)

Check that every paragraph focuses on one strand of the argument.

The first sentence of a paragraph should give 'clues' about its content. Get into the habit of thinking 'one paragraph, one idea'. (See also Suggestion 1 above.)

Ask your tutor whether copies of highly graded essays are available. If so, try to analyse them in the light of the above. Again, start by finding the main idea in every paragraph. You may feel defeated at first, but persevere. You will learn a lot about essay writing.

If you need more help, try the Dyslexia Support Co-ordinator and/or the study skills workshop.

4   Try to plan everything you write – from sentences to dissertations. Think before you write. This is neither as easy nor as obvious as it sounds.

Practise thinking/writing in short, complete sentences. Starting to write an open-ended sentence whilst hoping for inspiration isn't a good idea.

Get into the habit of reading each sentence aloud and by itself (from one full stop to the next). If it doesn't make sense, you need to think again. Read it slowly, two or three times if necessary.

Remember, every sentence needs a word of action (a verb). Most sentences also need a subject (the person or thing performing the action). (See examples in Appendix 12 on page 62.)

5   Whatever you are writing, you should consider your reader. Imagine yourself in his or her place. Is your writing well-structured and logical? Does it convey content effectively?

Are you sure that your reader is 'on the same wavelength'? *You* know where your argument is going but he or she may not. Explanations of 'obvious' connections within and between paragraphs/sentences are the writer's responsibility.

Writing is a craft. For most students it is also hard work. The best writers are very critical of their own performance. What exactly am I trying to say here? Could that sentence be more concise? In all honesty, am I making sense?

Some students find it hard to analyse their own writing. One way forward is to pretend that you are in a tutorial. Imagine your tutor asking you to explain/justify every sentence/connection.

6   Improve reading by learning when to read closely and when to scan. It is not always necessary to read every word. A quick scan of the text might suffice.

If you would like to improve your scanning skills, talk to the Disability Officer. Ask for a session with a specialist.

You may find it hard to change your habits but the first step is easy. Before you pick up a book, think about your reasons for reading. For example, do you need details or just a general impression? The first requires close and careful reading. A quick scan of the book's contents page will do for the second.

As with writing, you must be clear about your objectives. Forward planning, thinking and analysis are priorities.

7   Try to be positive about exams. You probably know more than you think. Again, you need to organize and prioritize. The syllabus/ course outline and past papers should inform your revision.

Be realistic about the time available and the nature of the task. Draw up a weekly timetable for all the subjects to be revised.

Generally, you should revise with a pen in your hand. Take notes/underline as necessary.

Set objectives for each session. For example, 'By the end of this session I will have invented/checked/rehearsed a mnemonic which defines ....' (See examples in Appendix 8 on page 55 and Appendix 14 on page 66.)

If you still feel unsure about revision, ask for advice from your Disability Officer.

8   Try to make best use of the library. Don't waste time stumbling around by yourself.

Take a list of the books and references you need. Library assistants are there to help, but you must help them first.

Ask about the facilities/indexing system. Be sure you know how everything works. Don't be shy about asking questions. From everyone's point of view, it is better to spend time now rather than waste it later.

Find out what are the busiest/quietest times. If possible, organize visits to suit the librarian.

9   Thinking about studying generally, what about your concentration? Work out when it's at its best/worst and adjust accordingly. Start to manage your concentration – no one can do it for you!

You might feel that you concentrate better in the library than at home. If so, you need to reorganize your timetable, social and family life.

Be honest – identify which distractions are the most difficult to ignore/resist. Take practical steps to avoid them.

10   Accept that studying is – largely – what you make it.

Think about the processes involved. When you study, you have to:

- take in ideas
- sort out the ideas in your mind
- express ideas clearly and concisely.

Study can be difficult and frustrating. It can also be exciting and rewarding.

11   Thinking of exam revision, don't forget the photocopier. It is very easy to enlarge important texts and notes. Often, this improves readability – even at a distance. Consider pasting these enlargements on walls and doors.

12 Regarding further feedback and help with spelling, see Chapter 1 suggestion 9 on page 6.

Summary

- Think about how you learn/write. Get into the habit of criticizing your own performance.

- Be positive about exams. Find the course outline and plan your revision.

- Spend time in the library. Practise finding 'your' section. Ask for help if you're unsure.

Chapter 3

Advice from other students

Reference: Questionnaire item 3: Assuming your own experiences have been fairly typical, what advice would you give to other dyslexics who are thinking of studying for a degree?

> Most replies gave very practical advice. Also, more than half the sample said that rewards outweighed the frustrations.

Suggestions from students (general)

1   Try not to panic. It won't be as bad as you think.

2   At the preliminary interview, ascertain from whom, what and where help is available.

3   Think seriously about the level of study. Would it be better to take a less ambitious course?

4   Don't choose anything that requires too much writing. Your written English is not always up to the task.

5   Know your own limits and difficulties. Allow that it will be harder for you than everyone else.

6   Go for it, but realize that you have to do a lot more work than the others. Don't expect help from course officials.

7   Get to know your lecturers. Discuss issues before they become problems.

8   Pick modules that are of interest rather than the easiest. Be prepared to argue the point.

9   Be open about dyslexia. Make sure your department understands the issues involved.

10   Find the people who want, and are willing, to help. It is important to keep going.

11   Put aside extra time for learning and learn from your mistakes.

12   Don't panic, and do control stress. I have found that when I panic the dyslexia becomes far worse.

On a more practical level, a personal computer (PC) was the favourite resource. One response is typical.

> It is worth pushing for access to a PC. Essays and spelling are so much easier. It's quite easy to learn the basics ... I couldn't believe the difference it made.

More practical advice from students follows.

1   When you're making notes, develop your own shorthand. Write up the notes properly later.

2   Take a tape recorder into lectures. Don't try to take notes, just sit and listen. Do proper notes later.

3   Make sure you have, and carry, a full psychological assessment to back you up. I have found it necessary.

4   Don't neglect yourself and make sure you get enough sleep. You need it more than most!

5   Never, ever, let piles of rough notes accumulate. Type them up as you go along. It's good revision anyway.

Although not advice as such, the rewards of learning were also mentioned.

> When you finally do produce something decent, the satisfaction is great.

> If you're really interested in what you're doing, it's tremendous.

> Graduation makes it all worthwhile.

> If you do your fair share of work, you should be OK. It's certainly worth it.

> It's not as difficult as it sounds. Be not afraid.

> Many people cope with disorder throughout life and at university and still achieve great success. Work round your dyslexia. It can be done.

> It all gets too much at times but, then again, it's marvellous when the light dawns!

Summary

Finally, do read and reread the above. These students speak from real experience. Their suggestions are sensible, sensitive and realistic.

Studying is liked and hated for similar reasons. It is hard work but – if you enjoy a challenge – it is very rewarding.

Chapter 4

Survival techniques

Reference: Questionnaire item 4: What resources, strategies and advisers have proved helpful in the day-to-day management of your course?

There was considerable emphasis on the advantages that technology can offer to people with dyslexia. Tape recorders for use in lectures and seminars, PCs with appropriate software, portable computerized note-takers and spell checkers were seen as a lifeline by many.

However, the majority were also aware of the importance of seeking advice and help from a wide range of people, from other students to professors. This is vital if things seem to be going wrong. The theme of individual strategies to develop useful study skills, maximize learning and make the best use of time also comes through very clearly.

Support via technology

I always record lectures. This means I only need to write down key points, which can be expanded from the tape later on.

I found out about this small, portable note-taker, which is easy to use. I take notes in lectures and I also use it to write down all sorts of things I might forget.

The computer is an invaluable resource for me as it allows a high degree of organization and presentation with much less effort.

My laptop is the best thing I've ever had. I use it for notes in lectures and it solves my problems with handwriting (which is awful). I can do several drafts of an essay and I can make sure that it looks good too.

I rely a lot on my spell checker. It seems to take the pressure off me when I use it.

My PC helps me with making notes. I can print them out on different coloured paper for different subjects and that's a real help to me in finding what I want at a glance. The colours help when I'm revising as well.

My PC is the best thing I've ever come across. But I needed some help to get the best out of it. For example, it has a program for spreadsheets and other business studies data.

Support from people

I was having awful problems and one of my lecturers said I might be dyslexic. She sent me along to the Disability Office to talk to them about it. They were really helpful and arranged for me to have a full assessment. At last, I realized that there were good reasons for the things I couldn't do; I wasn't either lazy or stupid! Everything started to get a lot better from then on.

I go to counselling and just talking it through with someone makes it easier to cope with the anxiety that can build up from time to time. The Disability Office also gives me personal support and they are very good at liaising with academic staff if that's needed.

It really helps to share your experiences with other students and to get some advice from them.

The one-to-one help I've had with reading and note-taking and with writing essays has got me through and I can pay for it from the DSA.

My professor was really sympathetic. He gave me tips on how to use my PC and told me to write everything down on it straightaway so as not to forget it. It works for me.

I made contact with my personal tutor in the early weeks of my first semester and I explained about my dyslexia. He made sure I get extra time in exams.... It's essential to sort out any problems early in your course.

I learned the hard way how important it is to communicate and to keep in touch with other people. Now I always check my e-mail and look in my pigeonhole for letters and marked essays. I keep an eye on noticeboards as well.

Personal strategies

I try to be as organized as possible. This means making 'to do' lists, which help me to plan my free time and to organize my academic work.

For me it's better to get an early start, so I often get up and do some reading or I plan an essay while I'm fresh. I also start on my assignments as early as possible in the semester. I've had to learn to avoid distractions too. I put a note on my door when I'm revising and I want to concentrate hard.

It's practical tips that I need and the Dealing with Dyslexia workshop is great for that. That's where I got the idea of colour coding my notes. I use colour too for different sections of essays at the planning stage. But I still have to allow a lot more time for work than other students do.

Suggestions

1   Check whether your college or university has PCs for students to use. Remember to make backup copies of your disks so as not to lose all your hard work.

2   Look to see if your dyslexia assessment report recommends
       that you should use any kind of 'assistive technology'.
       This covers PCs and laptops (standard and voice-
       activated), portable note-takers, scanners, tape recorders,
       dictaphones and so on. If you are eligible for the Disabled
       Students' Allowance (DSA), you can apply for funds to
       purchase your own personal equipment. If not, there may
       be technology you can borrow or access in some other
       way.

3   Does your assessment indicate that you would benefit from
       working with a specialist tutor? Do you need to dictate your
       answers to exam questions? You may be eligible for the
       DSA, which will cover all these costs.

4   Make an appointment to discuss any matters of this kind
       with Disability Office staff or with the Dyslexia Support
       Co-ordinator.

5   Always make sure you know how to get the best out of your
       equipment. Read the manual and check whether training
       is available. Ask for tips from staff and from other students.
       If you need more help, contact the Dyslexia Support
       Co-ordinator.

6   Be positive about your dyslexia and look for the help you
       need. Academic staff such as lecturers and personal tutors
       can provide a great deal of support. They can also help to
       make sure that the assessment of your work takes into
       account the effects of your dyslexia.

7   Remember that communication is very important. It is also
       a two-way process. So make sure you read noticeboards,
       check your pigeonhole and your e-mail, respond to written
       communications and turn up on time for lectures, seminars

and tutorials. Also, if you need to ask for help or advice, make an appointment in good time.

8   Try to tackle any problems early rather than late. For example, if you know you are likely to have difficulties with exams, find out what help might be available. Ask your personal tutor or contact the Dyslexia Support Co-ordinator.

9   Ask for help from your friends. They may remember things you have forgotten. You can also learn a lot just from talking together about the work you're doing.

10   If you start to feel under pressure, look for the help that is there. Get in touch with the Disability Office or with your personal tutor. Sessions with a counsellor may also be available.

11   Attend study skills workshops, especially those designed for students with dyslexia. You will pick up useful tips, try out different learning strategies and meet other dyslexic students too.

12   Check your dyslexia assessment report to see if it recommends individual learning support. If this is the case, the Disability Office may be able to put you in touch with a specialist tutor. They may also help you to claim the costs of this from the DSA.

13   Start to work out your own preferred learning style. For example, experiment with using different colours to help you recognize subjects, sets of notes, sections of an essay or report, chapters in a dissertation. Decide at what time of day you function best. Does it suit you best to do academic work early in the morning or late at night?

14   Plan your time carefully so that you can get the right balance between work and play. This is very important indeed, because you probably need to work longer and harder than other students – but you must set aside time to relax as well.

Summary

•   Start by finding out what support and advice is available and be prepared to talk to academic and support staff about your individual needs.

•   Make sure you manage your time to the best advantage, so that you have space for study and for leisure and relaxation. Try using assistive technology and see if you can get financial support such as the DSA to buy what you need.

•   Develop your own learning strategies so that you know how to use your strengths and cope with your weaknesses. Talk about your course and your problems with friends.

Chapter

Key resources

Reference: Questionnaire item 5: Given that resources are limited, which one resource would you prioritize and why?

This seems to have been a difficult question to answer and one that provoked much thought. However, the majority of responses fall into two main categories. Students are most appreciative of help from people, ranging from those willing to offer a sympathetic ear, to the guidance and support available from academic and specialist support staff.

Students tend to be most emphatic about the ways in which they value and, in some cases, really enjoy using technology, especially computers and a wide range of software. Resources such as these can help to lighten a heavy workload and significantly improve the planning and presentation of written work.

It is worth noting that when such improvements take place, students are likely to be awarded higher grades.

The following responses reflect the enthusiasm that many people feel when appropriate technological aids are put in place.

My key resource just has to be the computer. Spell checkers can be brilliant. But I find the grammar checker hard to use. There are loads of software programs you can find for help with specific subjects.

A computer. What else is there to say? Without it I couldn't access the Net and that's where I can search out information for my course.

Computers are good at sorting out so many problems. But you need easy access to them.

Computers are brilliant, once you know how to use them. They feel like a personal advice line. My computer makes me feel independent and I think I'm beginning to feel more confident in my own abilities as well.

I can produce good work on a computer. Somehow, I seem to be able to see most of my mistakes when they are up on the screen and I can put them right with the spell checker and the edit menu. No more crossings out. No more copying out and redrafting by hand. Computers are ace!

It's great to be able to produce a piece of work that looks decent. Without a computer I would never be able to create such a clear and precise layout, let alone correct a lot of basic errors.

I believe that it is essential for all dyslexic students to have their own computer. Then you can work in private whenever you want.

I don't know how I survived before I had my assessment for dyslexia and then got my computer. They help you with your work and they are fun to use. Now I can start off by putting down what I feel or think. Then I use the menus to put it all right and turn it into a proper piece of work. It still takes me a lot of time, but it's much quicker than doing it all, including endless corrections, by hand.

My PC is really good, but I also use a tape recorder and for me that's even more of a help. I function best in relation to things I hear. So I record just about everything, including ideas for an essay. I can play it back and improve on it and then use that as a basis for what I have to write. It's a great method.

I need to be sure that I understand the lectures. So I record them and then use the tape to make some concise notes. These form the basis of an essay plan. I file them along with my tapes and they help with revision too. Notes and tapes are the basis of all my work.

My life was changed the day I got my voice-activated PC. My writing is appalling and it's so slow. My spelling is even worse! Now, I speak to my computer and it prints what I say on the screen. Press another button and it will speak what I have 'written' back to me. It still feels like a miracle.

However, nearly all of those whose replies are quoted above, and many others too, strongly emphasized the need for human contact of various kinds.

In Freshers' Week, I went to the Disability Office and I was able to discuss my assessment and all my support needs. Really, it was that first meeting which made so many things clear for me.

My priority is time with people. My personal tutor is there to discuss all sorts of issues. If I need it, she will still help me to plan my work over a semester. In my first year, I used to try to get lecturers to look over a piece of work at the planning stage, just to make sure I was on the right lines and it really helped my confidence. I don't need to do that now.

Specialist one-to-one tutoring is what I need more than anything else at the moment. I've only just found out that I'm dyslexic and having someone who can help me to sort out strategies for my work is really great. We have identified the things I am good at. These are my strengths. We also know what my weaknesses are and that's what I'm trying to deal with now.

Library staff are the people who help me most because my main problem is that my reading is so slow. They have allowed me extra borrowing time and have shown me how to use the microfiche so that I can select what I really need from our long book-lists. They will always try to make time for you, but it's best if you can catch them when the library is quiet.

I can access the library directly on my networked PC. This means I can find out what books are on the shelves and which ones are out on loan. I can even renew books via the university network.

I think it's important that lecturers understand that dyslexia really does exist. That means I can feel reasonably comfortable about going to see them to discuss any problems I might have.

To get the support you need you have to be prepared to go and talk to people. The help is certainly there if you go and look for it.

My friends help me most. Two of them are dyslexic, but the others aren't. If I get stuck or really fed up there's always someone to talk to.

The dyslexia support tutor knows a lot about my sort of difficulties and he arranged for me to use my computer for my exams and I can have extra time as well.

Suggestions

1   Make sure that your college or university is aware that you are dyslexic. Be ready to pass on a copy of the written evidence of your disability and to discuss your needs in detail.

2   If you are unsure about whether or not you are dyslexic, contact your personal tutor or specialist staff in the Disability Office for advice.

3   Find out what computers are available on open access and, if you need it, ask at the Disability Office about training in their use.

4   Check your dyslexia assessment report to see if there is a recommendation for you to have your own computer or any other technological study aids. If so, make an

appointment to discuss your needs and apply for funds from the DSA.

5   Get information and advice about software packages that will suit your individual needs and match your course requirements from specialist staff in the Disability Office. (See also Appendix 13, page 63.)

6   Check on help available from your university library. You may be online for easy access to catalogues of books, journals, newspapers and many other sources of local, national and international information.

7   Look for the people who will give you the support and understanding you need. Many, but not all, lecturers are aware of the problems faced by dyslexic students. Specialist staff who provide support and guidance for people with dyslexia know about study techniques, students with disabilities, the widening range of assistive technologies and what might suit your needs. Disability support staff and university administrators know about any special procedures for the assessment of students with dyslexia.

8   Make time to make friends. You will be able to help each other.

9   Take full advantage of any opportunities to discuss your written work at the planning stage.

10   Contact the Dyslexia Support Worker for help in finding a specialist tutor and applying for DSA funding for this.

11   Find out what sort of procedures are in place for assessment which takes into account the effects of dyslexia.

Summary

- Let people know that you are dyslexic, this makes it easier for them to provide the support you need. Provide documentary evidence concerning your dyslexia, e.g. your dyslexia assessment report.

- Make sure you find out what is available to meet your own needs and the requirements of your course.

- Make contact with all the people who can help you: other students, departmental administrators, academic staff and specialist support staff.

Chapter 6

Assessment: coursework or examinations?

Reference: Questionnaire item 6: In universities and colleges of further education, assessment is normally based on coursework as well as examinations. Which would you prefer and why?

A notably large proportion of those who responded to our questionnaire made it clear that they would prefer coursework to exams. This is because they know they can take extra time to achieve the standards they aim for via coursework. This is very important for those who need to ensure that work is planned effectively and that spelling and other errors are recognized and corrected.

Even when extra time is allowed for exams, many respondents explained that they still felt themselves to be under great pressure.

Comments from those who prefer assessment by coursework

Coursework for me every time because exams only seem to highlight my negative points – not my actual knowledge of the subject. I'm used to working about twice as long as the others do to turn in a decent piece of work. I've always had to do that and I can get some good results.

In my assignments, I can take the time to correct my spelling and to get my phrasing right. In this way, I feel I can try to compensate for my dyslexia.

Coursework is definitely best, especially when you can get some help just to make sure that you really are on the right track. Then you can be sure that you can actually show your own abilities. For me, exams are always hit or miss. Anyway, they depend on your state of mind on a given day. There is so much that is beyond your control and that doesn't make for good work.

I like to be able to use a bit of creativity or to take a bit of a different perspective on a question. But you can only try that out in coursework. There just isn't any room for that kind of approach within the tight framework of an examination.

Coursework is manageable for me. The sheer stress of coping with exams makes my dyslexia much worse. I can totally misread a question and just throw marks away. Yet I know my stuff and I've got good marks for an essay on precisely the same topic... It's so frustrating.

I am in my final year now and I have just finished my dissertation. It was very hard work, but I actually enjoyed it. I wrote it in drafts, straight on to my PC, and I knew that I could get every spelling correct. I also knew that I could go over my structure until I was satisfied with it. I have not been asked to do a single correction or any rewriting. There's absolutely no way I could have achieved that in an exam.

I learn more things through coursework. I can usually take the time to make sure that what I want to say flows reasonably well. Then the reader can understand what I'm saying.

I can only opt for coursework. This is because the limited period allowed for writing in exams just does not allow a student with dyslexia to put down what they know in a good style. I know my memory lets me down and I can't wait for it to start working again. Then I get into a panic and either freeze up altogether or I just put down the first thing that comes into my head. Not a good way of working!

Given a choice, it would be coursework for me every time. I can access books at my leisure and plan my research and my reading over quite a long period. That's how I can produce some reasonable results and really feel that I'm demonstrating my understanding.

Often, I can't understand the questions in exams, so then I don't know which to choose. Of course you can't ask for any help. So that's why I do better with essays and assignments.

Coursework for me, and this is mainly because I can do more than one draft and I can make amendments. I feel more confident that lecturers will understand it when I produce work in this way. I seem to remember it better myself as well.

I prefer continuous assessment all the way through. More time and the freedom to use it allows me to demonstrate what I know. It also helps to take a break and then come back to the writing. You just can't do that in an exam.

Coursework is less stressful and that's what makes the difference for me. Then again, I know that my memory just doesn't work in certain ways and exams rely quite a lot on tests of memory don't they?

If you panic in an exam (and I have done that), you are lost and there is no way back. That's why coursework is best.

Other views

I don't really mind as long as there is a reasonable balance between the assessment of coursework and exams. If it's about half and half, I can cope.

Sometimes, I actually feel better doing exams. A touch more pressure seems to be good for me. I make a concentrated effort to get through the revision and to tackle all the required questions.

I think it depends on the subject and the types of question asked. For me, multiple-choice questions and most things to do with diagrams and formulas are fine. But essay questions let me down every time.

I'm lucky because part of my course is examined by the 'open book' method. That's great for me because getting the answers right depends more on intelligence and understanding than on memory.

I prefer a combination of coursework assessment and examination. I have to do a lot of essays and reports and that takes me ages. At least with exams you do the revision and then you get it over with.

I'm surprised to say that I choose exams. I think it's because I use things like bullet points and flow charts for revision and it really helps. I get extra time as well and that's a great help.

I feel OK with both methods of assessment. At my university, there are arrangements so that markers give people with dyslexia a fair deal. I don't get penalised for my wonky spelling and I have applied to use a PC for my next set of exams. I use it for all my other work, so why not for exams?

Suggestions

1   Find out what methods of assessment are used on your course. This is a question that can be asked on an Open Day visit or when attending an interview with an admissions tutor. If you prefer, you can write to the departments of your choice requesting the information by letter.

2   Check to see if there is any allowance for the effects of dyslexia when your written work is marked, either as

coursework or in exams. In line with their Equal Opportunities policies, a growing number of colleges and universities have developed special procedures for the academic assessment of students with disabilities, and this will include students who have dyslexia.

3   Make sure that any recommendations for educational, technological or individual personal support appearing in your assessment for dyslexia are acted upon. These can include extra time for exams, support from a specialist tutor, copies of lecture notes and transparencies for overhead projectors (OHPs), use of a PC and other aids, and so on.

4   Develop your own filing system in which to keep copies of the documents you will acquire as your course progresses. This information will be very useful in relation to your essays and assignments as well as for revision for exams. Try to organize it so that you can use it easily. For example, match the colour of a file to a subject or module. Use different coloured paper for different sets of notes. If you use tapes, file these, using labels and coloured stickers so that you can find them easily.

5   Store work that has been marked with the material on which it was based. This is invaluable for revision.

6   See Appendix 14 (page 66) for advice on revision and examination techniques.

7   Ask for timetables, essay and assignment questions at the beginning of each semester. This can help you to focus on what you have to produce for assessment.

8   Ask for book-lists before the beginning of a semester. If you are a slow reader, this can be really helpful (but remember to take notes and to file them!).

9   Always make notes or (if you are good at remembering what you hear rather than what you see) record the main points of the text onto tape.

10   Identify your sources on tape, just as you would on paper. For example, record the author's name, the title of the book or journal article, the date of publication and the number of the page from which the information or the quotation was taken.

11   Remember that deadlines for written work tend to cluster towards the end of a semester. So plan your time so that you can cope with this.

Summary

- Make sure you know what methods of assessment are used thoughout your course.

- Find out if there are any special procedures in place for the academic assessment of students with dyslexia.

- Check on the kinds of support recommended in your dyslexia assessment report and make sure that this is passed on to your department and to the Disability Office.

- Whenever possible, start your reading (and note-taking) in good time, even before the semester begins.

- Try using a tape recorder in lectures and seminars. It might also help you to tape your ideas and other things to remember, instead of writing them down.

- For revision, develop your own personal methods of storing copies of your completed written work. Include copies of questions, reading lists, handouts, copies of notes and OHPs.

Appendix

Financial support for students with dyslexia

- This information is for guidance only.

- For further information, see the publications mentioned below.

  In addition, see the list of Useful Addresses on pages 95 and 96.

- Contact your local education authority, college or university concerning your own individual needs.

What do colleges provide?

Open Learning Centres

Usually, study support for all students is to be found here. Specialist staff, experienced in working with people with dyslexia, may also be available.

Access Centres

Some colleges have an Access Centre on site. Here you can get advice and information, including costs, about a range of technological aids. These include PCs, printers, software and much else.

Counselling services

You may be referred for counselling to help you cope with stress or any personal problems arising from your dyslexia. This is normally free of charge and the service is confidential.

What do universities provide?

- Information and advice about individual support.

- Help from staff specializing in supporting students with disabilities, including dyslexia.

- Assistance in applying for funds, for example the Disabled Students' Allowance (DSA).

- Screening and diagnostic assessment for dyslexia.

- Possible loan of specialist equipment.

- Arrangements for extra time for examinations.

- Possible alternative methods of assessment.

- Accommodation with networked computer access.

- Free access to counselling service.

The Disabled Students' Allowance (DSA)

Students on full-time courses and those strudying part-time who have been assessed as dyslexic may be eligible to apply for DSA funding. This is intended to help you pay for the special support you need as a result of your dyslexia.

Some of your questions answered

- Undergraduates on full-time courses in receipt of a grant are eligible to apply for the DSA.

- From September 2000 a grant will be available for students studying part-time on degree courses.

- Students on a full-year paid sandwich course cannot apply.

- From September 2000, postgraduates are eligible for funding comparable to the DSA (check your own eligibility with your grant-awarding body and your department).

- The DSA is not means tested.

DSA funding for 1999/2000

Always check on the amounts because they change frequently.

Specialist Equipment Allowance: up to £4055 per course

Examples of what it might buy:

- portable spell checker and note-taker
- dictaphones and tape recorders
- PC or laptop
- scanner
- specialist software, e.g. voice-activated package

Non-medical Personal Helper Allowance: up to £10 250 per year

Examples of what it might pay for:
Salary costs for:

- sessions with a specialist tutor
- personal note-taker
- proof-reader

General Allowance: up to £1350 per year

Examples of what it might buy:

* textbooks
* batteries
* tapes
* coloured transparencies
* photocopying

How to apply

1   Write a letter of application to your local education authority (LEA).

2   Enclose a copy of an assessment of your dyslexia, no more than two years old.

3   Provide detailed supporting information from your University Disability Office or academic department.

4   Include specifications and prices of recommended technology.

5   Attach estimate of costs of specialist support.

6   Wait for a written approval of your request for funds.

What happens next?

If your request is accepted, you can then make arrangements to purchase what you require. Check on how to do this with your LEA and with your university. Always keep all invoices and receipts for purchase of goods and services, so that you can claim refunds.

Important points to remember

- The amount you receive will be based on the recommendations from your psychologist and from staff in the university.

- Make sure you have an appropriate warranty and/or insurance cover for servicing and breakdown.

- Apply as soon as you can, so that you will have the support you need at the beginning of your course.

- If you find out you have dyslexia only after your course has begun, you can still apply for the DSA.

Appendix 2

Financial support for students with dyslexia on healthcare courses

(Reference: Dyslexia: Screening and assessment (a basic guide), page xxiii)

Many universities now include Schools of Health Studies. Students on a range of full-time healthcare courses are usually funded in a variety of ways via an NHS bursary but financial support in relation to dyslexia is not available. Those studying part time are usually required to pay their own fees and again receive no funding for support in relation to dyslexia.

Some support for full-time students on degree courses who have dyslexia may be available. For further information, see the Useful Addresses list on pages 95 and 96. In addition, always contact your own university about your individual needs.

Where to find out more

Publications

- *Bridging the Gap:* a guide to the Disabled Students' Allowance (DSA) in higher education in 1998/99, available from your local education authority or the Department of Education and Employment (tel: 0800 731 9133).

- *Financial Help for Health Care Students:* available from NHSB Department of Health, PO Box 410, Wetherby LS23 7LN.

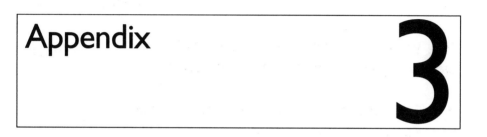

Appendix

(Reference: Chapter 2, Suggestion 1, page 10)

Example: common abbreviations (note-taking)

The following are widely used and recognized:

1	∴	=	therefore
2	∵	=	because
3	⊃	=	implies
4	>	=	greater than
5	<	=	less than
6	≠	=	does not equal
7	eg	=	for example
8	cf	=	compare
9	nb	=	note well
10	ie	=	that is
11	wd	=	would
12	cd	=	could
13	shd	=	should
14	b/4	=	before
15	~	=	about/approximately

Also, your course will have its own high-use words. Invent and practise useful abbreviations. For instance:

-     Ec. Consids. = economic considerations
      Hum.   = humanities.

Appendix 4

(Reference: Chapter 2, Suggestion 1, page 10)

Exercise: note-taking

1   Read 'Railways' (below).

2   Make notes bearing in mind that:
    (i)   notes should be well spaced and legible
    (ii)   you must date your notes and record your source/title
    (iii) you should abbreviate words/phrases where possible
    (iv)   many writers give the general theme in their opening sentence
    (v)   (in this instance) four specific aspects of the general theme might be identified. Brief illustrations of a point are often helpful.

When you have finished, evaluate your notes and compare them with those on page 49. Check for similarities and differences.

The basic principles mentioned above can be used in many other note-taking situations.

Railways*

The railways, beginning in earnest in the 1830s, had a permanent and far-reaching influence on village life. Their life-giving injection of cheap and rapid transport revived old, decayed fishing harbours like Grimsby; turned seaside villages into ship-building centres and resorts, like Barrow-in-Furness and Southend;

converted tiny, inland route centres into railway towns, the home of engine works like Crewe, Swindon, Wolverhampton, Norwich, Worcester and Ashford. The scenery itself was changed. To secure the easy gradients demanded by railway engineers, great embankments and high viaducts were thrown across wide valleys, soaring bridges made light of deep river barriers, and tunnels, their portals massively decorated with turrets and battlements, penetrated steep hillsides. Little hamlets of railwaymen grew up around the stations, which were generally a mile or two from the centre of the villages they served. These new communities were related to existing villages, because railways served as major outlets for farm commodities and as a means of obtaining fertilizer and farm equipment. Slow, passenger trains, stopping at country halts, provided a new, and eventually cheap, way of getting to market towns, and there was the occasional excursion trip to the seaside or beauty spot. The poorest class of villagers, however, the farm labourers, began to enjoy the advantages of railway travel only towards the end of the century, when wages had risen and the fares had come down. But long before this the railways had offered the village lads a more attractive means of employment, and country men made up a fair proportion of the quarter of a million employed by the railways in the 1870s.

Though railways offered a new field of employment, they also destroyed an old one. The advent of cheap, fast, railway travel spelled the early demise of the coaches. Within a few years it was no longer possible for the roadside cottager to set his clock by the passing of the mail, or for country children to wait excitedly for the great event of the stage's appearance, emerging suddenly over the brow of the hill with whip cracking and steam rising from the horses.

*From Mingay (1999), cited in Heaton and Mitchell (1999) (see also *Helpful books* in *References and resources*, pages 94 and 95).

'Railways' model answer (attempt by experienced student)

Source Mingay (14/11/96)
Railways

Gen influence vill life

(i)   commncs

(ii)   indust + comm dvlpt

(iii)   new twns at route centres

1   Scenery

(i)   landscape alters – cf eng'rs

(ii)   embanks, viaducts, bridges, etc.

2   New stations

(i)   created own hamlets

(ii)   linked with exist vills

3   Passenger traffic

(i)   easy journeys – opps wk + trade

(ii)   recreatn

4   Employment

(i)   increase – new jobs railway

Appendix 5

(Reference: Chapter 1, Suggestion 7, page 4)

Example: note-taking style ('spider' plan/mind mapping)

Source: lecture on note-taking, 14/5/98 by FRL

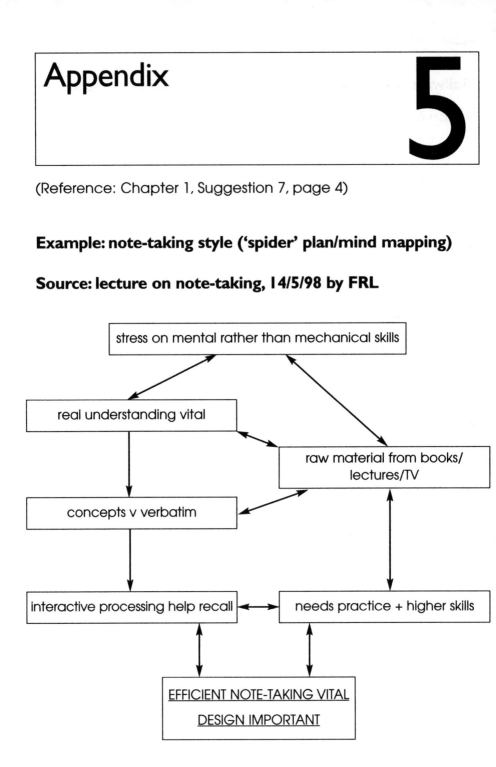

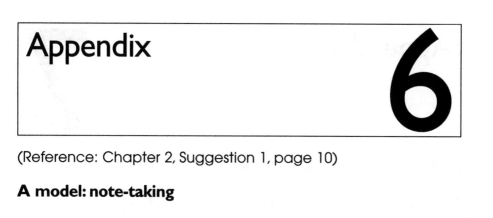

Appendix 6

(Reference: Chapter 2, Suggestion 1, page 10)

A model: note-taking

EXTERNAL KNOWLEDGE
(THE TEXT, THE TV, THE LECTURE)

INTERACTIVE NOTE-TAKING
USE YOUR OWN WORDS
(THEN YOU WILL 'OWN' THE LANGUAGE AND IDEAS OF THE
ORIGINAL WRITER/SPEAKER)

INTERNAL KNOWLEDGE
(THE KNOWLEDGE/EXPERIENCE IS STORED FOR FUTURE RECALL)

Appendix

(Reference: Chapter 1, Suggestion 7, page 4)

Example: formal writing and basic referencing

Notice:

1   No short forms (*is not** rather than *isn't*, for example)

2   No first person (*it seems*** rather than *I believe*, for example see page 53)

3   Use *and so forth/and so on**** rather than *etc.*, see page 53.

4   Usually, references are numbered and listed at the end of an essay, but check this; your tutor might suggest a different style.

Essay title: The ability to use language to communicate is essential for successful social interaction. Discuss.

If successful social interaction is defined in terms of achieving communicative objectives, the motorist with upraised fist must be seen as an effective communicator: both he and the overtaking taxi driver understand the context and the unambiguous message.

Having said that, their 'communication' is not* 'a sharing of ideas' (1) or 'common intercourse'. The abbreviated social exchange is 'going nowhere' and its success is, therefore, limited. The intercourse between mother and baby shares some of the characteristics of this unsatisfactory communication: the baby may or may not be as egocentric as the grimacing motorist (and this is discussed below) but his means of communication are similarly primitive. In both cases, restricted social interaction is linked to limited linguistic expression. That is not to say that real communication is exclusively language-based or that linguistic and communicative skills are one and the same. On the other hand, as Greene (2) points out, it is difficult to imagine that either a society's or individual's potential could be achieved without language. Both spoken and written forms of language are central to the development of microcosm and macrocosm, spoken language being of particular interest here.

Confusingly, definitions of language are numerous. It seems** that language is a universal human (as opposed to animal) activity. It can be used internally and reflectively or for the external expression of ideas, opinions and so forth.*** It is also a bonding agent in that it is shared and understood by communities of language speakers. Language is a repository for the stock of common knowledge. Additionally, as Heaton (3) points out, language also has its own infrastructure and conventions. Perhaps most importantly (in this context) language is inextricably intertwined with learning, thought, cognition, intelligence and social interaction.

Referencing (see point 4 above)

Notice: the list gives author's name, year of publication, title of book and publisher. Thus:

1   Gowers Sir E (1984) *The Complete Plain Words*. Penguin Books.

2   Greene J (1990) *Introduction to Psychology*. Open University.

3   Heaton, P (1986) *Dealing with Dyslexia*. Whurr Publishers Ltd.

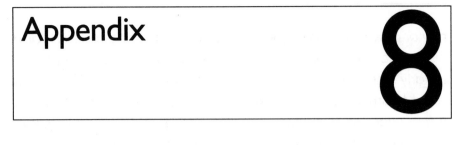

Appendix 8

(Reference: Chapter 1, Suggestion 9, page 6)

Examples: aids to memory (mnemonics)

The linking and associating power of the memory can be used in many different ways. Funny/silly/rude mnemonics work well.

Consider the following examples and then invent some of your own.

Spelling mnemonics

1 Be**au**tiful

Link the 'hard' part of this word (**e a u**) to associated initial letters:

beautiful **e**lephants **a**ren't **u**gly.

2 Li**ai**son

Link the 'hard' part of this word (**i a i**) to associated initial letters:

liaison **i**s **a**n **i**dea.

3 Amat**eur**

Link the 'hard' part of this word (**e u r**) to associated initial letters:

amateur team's **e**ntry **u**pset **R**angers!

4   Success

Link the 'hard' part of this word (**c c s s**) to associated initial letters:

↓ ↓ ↓↓

To be a su**cc**e**ss**,
you need double C and double S.

*Definition mnemonics**

The idea of memorizing bits of information by linking them with things that are easier to remember has a long history.* Think of EGBDF (the lines of the musical staff) for example; many people have memorized these by linking them with the phrase **E**very **G**ood **B**oy **D**eserves **F**ootball. The method seems to work even though there are no obvious connections between football, boys and music!

The mnemonic principle can also be applied to definitions.

Example:

Imagine that you are a psychology student preparing for an exam. You know that you must learn and remember a definition of the term **behaviourism.**

Step 1

Write what you need to remember: in this case,

BEHAVIOURISM IS THE **S**TUDY **O**F **A**CTUAL **R**ESPONSES.

Step 2

Try and make links as mentioned above.*

Here, as the initial letters of the 4th, 5th, 6th and 7th words spell **SOAR**, the phrase **BEHAVIOURISM SOARS** might help you remember the definition. (Notice; the mnemonic need not be 'sensible' to be effective.)

Step 3

Say the phrase/mnemonic out loud a few times. Using this example see if you can recall what the word **SOAR** represents/has links with: BEHAVIOURISM = **S**tudy **o**f **a**ctual **r**esponses.

If you fail the first time, try again; your performance will almost certainly improve.

Now choose a definition of your own and work through Steps 1, 2 and 3.

Step 4

Test yourself at increasingly longer intervals: 1 hour, 6 hours, 1 day, 3 days and so on.

Finally:

You may feel that all this is more trouble than it's worth but there is plenty of evidence to suggest that these methods work. More advice on **memory training** can be found in *Use your Head* (Buzan 1990). (See section on *Helpful books* in the *References and resources* on pages 94 and 95.)

Appendix

(Reference: Chapter 1, Suggestion 11, page 6)*

Examples: Find your own learning style

1   I like the challenge of new and different things.

2   I prefer thinking things through before coming to a conclusion.

3   I don't find it easy to think of wild ideas off the top of my head.

4   I love lots of information – the more I have to sift through the better.

5   If I'm writing a formal letter, I try out several rough drafts first.

6   I like to consider all my options before making up my mind.

7   I don't like creative ideas. They aren't very practical.

8   It's best to look before you leap.

9   I do whatever I need to, to get the job done.

10   I like to find out how things work.

* Note: If you would like to know more about this type of test see page 6.

Appendix

(Reference: Chapter 2, Suggestion 3, page 11)

Examples: link words and phrases

These words help readers to follow your ideas. They give a sense of direction. Link words are your reader's 'signposts'.

Set 1: Developing an argument
Furthermore
In addition to
Moreover
Similarly
Supplementary evidence suggests

Set 2: Changing the direction of an argument
However
In clear contrast to this
Nevertheless
On the other hand
So far the emphasis has been upon

Set 3: Link words/phrases (general)
It is important to remember
It is worth noting
Other views merit consideration
Unfortunately the reality is rather different

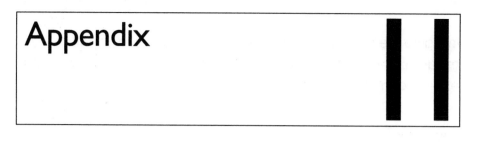

Appendix

(Reference: Chapter 2, Suggestion 3, page 11)

Examples: key words in essay titles

Essay titles often include key words listed below. Check their precise meaning. This will help you to plan/develop your argument.

Compare and contrast

Look for – and stress – both similarity and unlikeness. Perhaps, reach a conclusion about which is better/preferred.

Imagine comparing and contrasting England and France. You could write first about contrasts in language and food. Similarities could then be discussed: both are European countries, each has a mixed economy and so forth.

In this example, your conclusion might mention the Channel Tunnel. You could discuss the effects of this. You might argue that closer links will reduce contrasts and encourage similarities.

Criticize

Give your judgement about the merit of opinions/arguments/ theories. Support your judgement by discussing the relevant evidence/reasoning.

Define

State the precise meaning of a word/phrase. Sometimes, the *Oxford English Dictionary* is a good starting point. You may need to give more than one definition. You might be expected to provide more than one example.

Imagine defining the word 'precious'; you could mention both modern and traditional meanings. The reader would probably expect examples in context.

Describe

Give a detailed account in narrative form. Before you begin, consider the main characteristics – think of the way a good novelist builds/describes a central character.

Discuss

This word generally suggests a debate.

Imagine the title: Changes in licensing laws have ruined family life: discuss. You would consider this from two opposing points of view. Evidence is expected. You must sift/debate as you write. Discuss means that detailed arguments are required.

Evaluate

You must decide whether something is true/useful/worthwhile. Consider the evidence and reach a conclusion. (Approach as if a 'Discuss' essay – see above.)

Explain

Make plain/give reasons for something. For example: 'Explain why the car industry has flourished whilst railways have deteriorated'.

You might identify/write about/give examples of particular social/economic/political factors.

Illustrate

Make clear by describing examples/providing graphs/diagrams/ figures.

Interpret

Show that you understand. Explain the meanings or possible meanings. Before you start, check that you are clear in your own mind. Explain your terms of reference – 'where you are coming from'. Try to be very precise and explicit.

Justify

Show good grounds for something – maybe a decision. Think of/anticipate the likely objections. ('Of course, some experts would disagree because ... but the evidence is clear...'.) Always try to describe and answer the opposition's case!

Outline

Give the main features of something. Omit minor details. Emphasize structure and arrangement.

Relate

Use essay form/formal style* but act as 'narrator'. Show how things are connected. Describe how they are alike/affect each other.

*Formal style is explained in Appendix 7, page 52.

Appendix 12

(Reference: Chapter 2, Suggestion 4, page 12)

Examples: sentences

Many students recognize 'sensible' sentences by instinct. They may not know the rules of grammar but they know what 'feels right'.

The sentences below are grammatically correct. They are self-contained units of sense. If you read them out loud, they should sound complete. (If you are still unsure after reading these aloud, you may need help from an expert. Ask the Study Skills tutor for advice.)

Each sentence has:

- a subject (a person/thing performing an action)

- a verb (a word of action).

Simple active sentences

1   *Pam ran* to the shop.

2   *They drove* to the pub.

3   *The majority rejected* the evidence.

4   *Examination Boards are* concerned about standards.

5   *Libraries are struggling* to cope with demands.

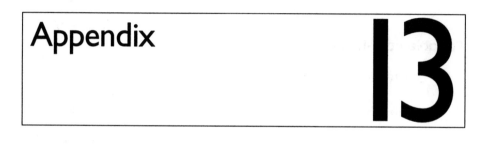

Appendix

13

(Reference: Chapter 5, Suggestion 5, page 31)

Assistive technology

Many students with dyslexia find that using technology is a very good way of improving the production of academic work.

Most colleges and universities now have word processors and printers available free for student use, but access is not always easy when everyone else on the course seems to want to use the equipment at the same time. To help with this, many universities now make some PCs available for the use of students throughout the day and night.

However, a growing number of those assessed as dyslexic are recommended to use a range of technology suited to their own individual requirements. In many cases, this can be funded through the DSA. (See Appendix 1, page 40 for details.)

Examples of technology that might help you

Portable spell checker

*   Lightweight and battery powered

*   Many versions

*   Try out to see which best suits your needs

Portable note-taker

- Lightweight, battery and/or mains

- Looks like the keyboard of a computer, with a very small screen

- Will take up to 60 pages of notes in lectures or from books

- Includes spell checker

- Can be connected to a PC or Apple Mac to create normal files

Tape recorder

- Battery or mains

- Check on type suitable for your specific needs

- Can be used in lectures, seminars and to record your own ideas, information

Word processor (basic)

- Various specifications

- Check to make sure it meets your needs

- Ensure compatibility with existing college or university systems

- Includes spell checker and capacity to create your own personal dictionary of hard-to-spell or specialized words

- Check for facility to change screen background colours, fonts and size of print

- Software packages, such as the most recent version of Microsoft Office, usually included with no charge

- Should also include package to produce spreadsheets, databases and statistics

Additional specialist equipment

Voice-activated software

- Enables you to dictate to a PC that will put your words on screen and speak them back to you

Text reader

- Will read aloud the printed word

- Readings can be recorded on audio tape for future use

Access to the Internet

- For information, research

Things to watch

- Make sure you get reliable advice about what to buy.

- Your college or university may employ specialist staff who can advise you on specifications, funding and purchases.

- You may be required to attend an Access Centre for advice concerning specifications and purchases paid for via the DSA.

- Seek training so that you can maximise the use of your equipment.

- Check to see if IT courses are available to update your knowledge.

- Make sure you have appropriate insurance and warranty agreements in case of breakdown.

Appendix 14

(Reference: Chapter 2, Suggestion 7, page 13 and Chapter 6, Suggestion 6, page 37)

Revision and examination techniques

- Are you nervous about taking examinations?

- Do you usually get better grades for coursework than for exams?

- Does your dyslexia assessment report indicate that you have problems with your short-term memory?

If you have answered YES to these questions, you may find the following recommendations to be helpful.

Stage 1: Check up on your support needs

- Has extra time for exams been recommended?

- Do you need to use a PC?

- Do you need to dictate your answers?

Stage 2: Using your memory

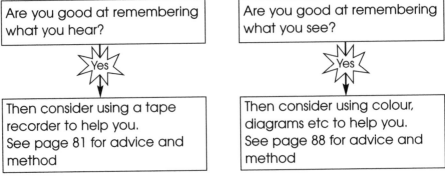

Are you good at remembering what you hear?	Are you good at remembering what you see?
↓ Yes	↓ Yes
Then consider using a tape recorder to help you. See page 81 for advice and method	Then consider using colour, diagrams etc to help you. See page 88 for advice and method

Stage 3: Guidelines for successful revision

- Make sure you know well in advance when and where your exams will take place.

- Keep copies of all course documents, essay questions, reading lists and marked work.

- Make this material the basis of your revision.

- Get copies of past papers from your department or library.

- Compare your work with questions asked on past papers.

- Review your assessed work and select that with the best grades.

- At this stage it is vital to make sure that you revise enough material to cover the questions that are likely to be asked.

- If you decide to expand on what you have got, look at your less successful papers and see if you can improve them by filling in gaps in knowledge or correcting mistakes.

- If you are desperate for additional material, look back through your notes, tapes, handouts. Use them to write up extra material relevant to likely questions.

- Reduce each piece of work into notes (written or on tape).

Stage 4: Exam practice

- Choose a question from a past paper.

- Work through your batch of relevant material.

- Time yourself to answer the question in one hour.

- Consider extending this, so that you can be sure that you can write for up to three hours at a stretch.

Stage 5: Taking the exam

- Make sure you arrive on time.

- Remember to bring more than one pen and a reliable watch.

- Take time to read all the instructions on your paper.

- Select and mark the questions you are going to answer.

- Questions may be answered in any order, as long as they are clearly numbered. So start off with something you feel confident about.

- Allocate your time as equally as possible between the questions.

- If you have not completed a question when your allocated time is up, you must move on to the next question. Leave space to use later.

- Remember that grades are calculated on an average of all marks, so make an attempt to answer all the required questions.

Stage 6: The last few minutes

- Go quickly through what you have written.

- Correct any errors you can see.

- Add any extra information in brief (notes or diagram).

- Remember that the last paper you sit is just as important as the first, so try to sustain your energy and your determination all the way through.

Appendix

Case history 1

Introduction

An ex-student of the authors, who graduated nearly 10 years ago, generously agreed to help with this book. What follows is largely his own work, though permission to edit was freely given. We feel that his first-hand account of his life to date will inspire and inform other students with dyslexia.

Background

For as long as I can recall I seemed to be different from other kids. I have always understood – and been able to build – things that work. Even when I was very young I could build Lego models with moving parts and make them work.

My father was a technology teacher so I had no shortage of real tools and I progressed from Lego to wood and metal. Together, my dad and I built customized bicycles with suspension and extra-low gears, a sidecar for my bike and a catamaran – this last was made from two canoes! I felt comfortable with this sort of activity. I was the only kid I knew who could borrow something, use it, do it up and return it in better condition! You would have thought that I couldn't have had it so good and you would be right if it wasn't for the fact that I had to go to school. From the age of 6, school put me in position where I failed even though I felt that I should be one of the high achievers. My practical skills didn't count for anything in school and my reading, writing and spelling abilities were very poor.

One peculiar thing that I remember is that more effort usually produced poorer grades – spend half the time and double the marks or spend twice as long and get half the marks. I still haven't worked that one out!

Obviously, my mum and dad knew that something was wrong and they worried because I hated school so much. I was labelled lazy and disruptive and once you are perceived in this way you are on a slippery slope. My parents knew that I was bright and capable but also that I was failing badly at school. From about 8 onwards I was regularly sent for tests of eyesight, hearing and intelligence. All the results suggested that I was perfectly normal.

My mum and dad spent hours trying to encourage me to read for fun but to this day I have read only one book for pleasure.

One of the biggest breakthroughs in my life was back in 1981. I was introduced to the school's first computer. It was a Sinclair ZX80 with a massive 1 K of RAM. From the moment I saw this small, white electronic box that displayed text on a flickering screen I was mesmerized. I can remember playing Lunar Landings, a game where you had to type in how much fuel you wanted to use to slow down the Lander to stop it crashing into the moon. Within half an hour or so, I was wanting to know how it worked and I discovered the computer program for the game. That meant that I knew how much fuel the game started with and I increased it to make the game easier! That was my first taste of computer programming.

From that moment I started struggling to read about anything to do with computers. I subscribed to Your Computer magazine (I still have the first copy) and read it religiously. This did more for my reading than anything. At this stage, all I wanted to do was eat and sleep computing. I wanted my own computer and was so keen that my parents did a deal and said that whatever money I could raise, they would double it. I sold my motor bike and did up and sold a number of bicycles. I managed to raise £200, which my parents doubled. I bought a Sharp MZ80 K computer in December 1982. At that time, the Sharp was the Rolls Royce of computers and I loved it.

By now, I was a fairly competent programmer and I spent some time in video arcades watching the games – not playing, just watching. I would then go home and write my own version of Tank Commander, Defender, Frogger or whatever.

Also at this time, I was being assessed by the school's psychologist, who said that I couldn't spell and that my handwriting was poor. He put me on the school's remedial spelling course but neither my self-esteem nor my literacy showed much improvement.

Recognition

My mum says that, for her, the breakthrough came when she read something about a dyslexia meeting to be held locally. She said the description of a dyslexic could have been written about me. Mum went to a meeting and came away convinced that I was dyslexic. She arranged for me to be assessed privately. I recall doing the intelligence tests and being told that I wasn't 'thick' but dyslexic. I cried for joy. There was a reason for my poor English. From that moment I never looked back.

I had private lessons with a specialist in dyslexia. As my main problem by then was spelling, she taught me how the English spelling system worked. There were rules that worked with families of words. Each week I would learn a rule/spelling pattern and apply it to worksheets, word searches and so forth. We also worked with cut-up letters and sentences. I think the tactile experience makes the letters more physical and, somehow, more meaningful.

Taught in this way, my spelling did improve and, partly as a result of this, I was moved into the O level stream. I managed eight O levels, all above grade C – including English. Luckily for me, the new GCSE was graded partly on coursework and partly on exam. I'm sure that I would have failed if everything had depended on the exam!

I then went on to take three A levels (physics, maths and computing), all of which I passed.

I don't know why, but at this point I became very interested in psychology. Through reading various psychology books, I began to understand why my specialist tutor's methods had worked while conventional teaching had failed. First, the tutor has to understand the problem and work out a solution/appropriate remediation. Next, the learner has to practise the new 'behaviour' at regular intervals. The time between increases as the memory impression deepens. Take, for example, the spelling rule about doubling the final consonant at the end of the root word. First, you learn the rule, then you work through some examples immediately and then again at the end of the session. After that, you follow up with related homework, which reinforces the same rule. After that and with any luck the rule is committed to long-term memory!

You will gather that I was beginning to use my strengths to overcome my weaknesses. The main problem at this point was my poor handwriting – often criticized. An obvious solution was to write a word processor program for my ZX Spectrum computer and build a printer port to allow a full-size dot matrix printer to be attached. In the event, this killed two birds with one stone. It gave me a computer studies project for my A level course and also the means to produce word-processed physics notes. Also, from time to time I sold these to students who had missed their lessons!

One thing that developed steadily throughout these years was a strong determination to succeed. I am sure this comes from my earlier failures so, maybe, there are advantages to being dyslexic.

Further progress

At the age of 14, my interests centred round computer programming and Lego! From this unlikely mix I was inspired to produce a computer controlled Lego lathe that turned candles into different shapes, as programmed into the computer. Little did I know that this project alone would open up so many opportunities later in life.

It was the start of my first serious entrepreneurial activities. Showing the lathe to people in the local technical colleges, it became apparent that there was a market opportunity for this. The technical training of students to program Computer Numerical Controlled (CNC) machine tools was all the rage. Usually, colleges would pay about £6000 for a single, small lathe to teach on. The ideal option would be to have 30 lathes, one for each student in the class. With my Lego lathe, this became a realistic option as 30 of mine cost less than one of theirs!

The possibilities looked good but I still knew very little about business. As I was still at school I teamed up with a one-man start-up company who wrote educational software. The plan was that he would manufacture the lathe electronic interface and copy the control software. Thinking everything was as it seemed, I contacted the head of Lego UK who was responsible for selling Lego to education authorities. He came to see the lathe in operation and we discussed sales and marketing strategies. He arranged for Lego to look at creating a lathe kit; my partner and I would supply the control electronics and software.

Unfortunately for me, it all went wrong but I did learn a lot about business and how it works. To cut a long story short, the partnership failed though the Lego connection was maintained.

The year I was 17, the government launched an Industry Matters initiative. Its objective was to try to attract the best students into industry rather than law and accountancy. One of the initiatives involved groups of A level students meeting leading local industrialists to learn what careers their particular industry had to offer.

About 10 students were chosen from each of the local sixth form colleges and I was lucky enough to be one of the group from our college. By this time I was beginning to have some idea of how the world worked and I prepared a set of photographs of my Lego lathe and took them to the meeting. The story soon spread and before I left I had secured a university sponsorship with a national glassware manufacturer and had offers from other industrialists to visit their factories.

Even better in some ways, a week later I was contacted by the managing director of a small company. He had heard about the Lego lathe and he offered me a part-time job. I worked weekends and any half-days off from college. The company made servomotors for industrial control applications. This was great for me as it combined all my hobbies: electronics, software and mechanics.

I had another stroke of luck while I was there. I discovered the firm's old NC machine that had to be programmed using punched tape; it was unbelievably slow and error-prone. I went to my boss and told him that for £20 (which I thought was a lot of money at the time) and using the company BBC Micro, I could convert his old NC machine to CNC. He laughed, put his hand in his pocket, threw me £20 and said, 'good luck'. He really didn't think I could do it, because a commercial CNC upgrade would cost about £6000. Within a week I had the machine running. This was a big turning point because from then on my boss took my ideas seriously.

At this time I was watching the way a Sheffield company was developing an electronics and software control system. Again I approached my boss and said that I could build a control system based on a BBC Micro. When it was finished, it worked so well that we started to manufacture my new commercial control system and the contract with our former supplier was terminated.

The 'reward' for all this was a university sponsorship worth £6000 per annum plus expenses.

University

I had set my sights on Hull University because I wanted to study electronics control and robotic engineering. I further developed my electronics and software skills and was awarded a 1st for my project and a 2:1 Honours degree.

By now my dyslexia was less of a problem. I made all my lecturers aware of my condition and used an Amstrad PC for my coursework. I used the spell checker and made sure that my work was always well presented, clear and accurate.

I also developed techniques for surviving lectures. Note-taking was a problem, as the lecturers spoke too quickly. If I tried to keep up, my writing (never good) became illegible so I started to write less and in capital letters. That way I could always read what I had written and so could everyone else. Further, I wrote on one side only of my (A4 paper) pad – I never wrote on the back. That way, I was always writing on my pad and this improves my writing.

I also concentrated on improving my strategies for revision. When it came near exam time, I would start my revision six weeks before the first exam. The first task was to plan my revision programme. I divided the day into five 50-minute slots, each with a 10-minute break. Each slot would then be allocated a subject and a specific number of topics on that subject. I would plan out the whole six weeks before I started. Remembering what I had been taught about learning and recall, I would go over difficult concepts again and again at increasingly longer intervals.

I found these methods worked extremely well for me. First, it gave me a good structured plan to work to – I did not allow extra time for difficult topics because I wanted to have time to revise topics on which I knew I could do well. Second, this scheme gave me defined chunks of time with a definite end. I could concentrate intensely for 50 minutes and if my concentration faltered I remedied that by reminding myself that the end (and a break) was in sight! Again, this all comes from my earlier lessons when I was specifically taught how to learn.

Latest situation

After graduating at 22, I became a director of the company that had sponsored me. I was content to hone my commercial skills and I left only when the company hit hard times in 1996.

I then joined an electronics design consultancy and became involved in developing mobile phones, digital TVs and wireless network products for household names. Once more, my dyslexia wasn't really a problem. In fact, it was not until recently that one of our directors mentioned it. Apparently, he had recognized the characteristic drive and determination and odd spellings in my e-mail!

The future

I am by most measures successful. I have a good salary and everything that goes with it. I also have a wonderful wife and I have never been happier or more confident. Money is no longer the big motivator; it just gives me the freedom to make choices.

All this is a far cry from those painful schooldays before my specific problems were recognized. Thanks mum and dad for not giving up on me – it's taken a while but I think I finally made it!

Appendix 16

Case history 2: a success story

Dr Mike Page recently gained a PhD for his thesis 'The role of penal policy in the reduction of political violence'. In his own words, he explains how he, as a person with dyslexia, gained his qualification.

Getting the letters

Having failed to achieve the results my teachers felt I was capable of achieving in my O level examinations, at the age of 16, I was sent to the local authority's educational psychologist for an examination. He identified that I showed signs of having a dyslexia-related condition known as Specific Learning Difficulty.

This created some problems for me because public understanding of dyslexia was still limited at this time. The belief that dyslexia meant stupid was widely held by many people, including teachers. Indeed, many argued that dyslexia was simply a new middle-class way of describing educational underachievement. Being a child of middle-class professionals, I fitted these criteria exactly.

Therefore my stated aim of going on to university was seen as unrealistic in the extreme. Even I did not dare say that my real aim in life was to try to get a PhD – one of the highest degrees available in the UK. The idea would have seemed absurd in the extreme – yet 13 years later I am sitting here writing this article as Dr Page.

How did I manage to get to this position? The reality is that I benefited from a mixture of goodwill, friendship, good luck and a stubbornness, which at times has verged on bloody-mindedness. The most important aspect came from the goodwill of the educational institutions where I have studied and the willingness of friends to help proof-read my work.

The form of specific learning difficulty from which I suffer manifests itself in difficulty with remembering arrays of letters or numbers. To this day, I cannot remember any phone numbers other than my own and that of my parents. This is easily dealt with by the use of an address book, but in spelling and arithmetic I still have problems. This is where good luck has come in. Modern technology, in the form of word processors and calculators, has benefited me greatly.

I am also one of the few people who can say that I have benefited from Northern Ireland's 'troubles'. By 1986, when I had finally achieved success in my school exams through the use of a scribe, few universities were willing to take me on.

However, the University of Ulster had grave problems recruiting students despite its good academic reputation. Many students from Northern Ireland chose to study in Britain or the Irish Republic, while few people from there would even consider studying in what was to them a war zone. This meant that my somewhat tarnished school results were sufficient to get me a place at the University of Ulster's Coleraine campus. Ulster was to leave an important mark on me. Not only was I treated by academics and fellow students as their intellectual equal for the first time, but I also developed a love for Irish Studies and specifically Northern Irish politics.

With the help and understanding of my teachers who, when they realized my problems, were willing to judge my work on its content rather than its form, I graduated with an upper-second-class degree, which gave me a place on the Masters course at the University of St Andrews – one of the institutions that had refused to touch me four years earlier. From that point, technology and friends together ensured that I had no problem in achieving first an MPhil and then, a few years later, my PhD, and therefore had no need to call on this University's Disabilities Unit, which I know provides first-class support for dyslexic students.

So now, at the age of 29, while I shall no doubt continue to have some problems with my written English, I am in a position where my specific learning difficulty has not prevented me achieving one of the highest degrees in the country. I am now ready to put it behind me and go on to live the rest of my life without any hang-ups about my intelligence or my academic ability.

Appendix 17

Building on your strengths

Karen and her memory

Are you good at remembering what you hear?

Many students who have dyslexia find that they can remember what they hear better than what they see. (The assessment report provided by your psychologist should normally make it clear if your short-term auditory memory is more reliable than your short-term visual memory.)

Read about Karen to see how she found ways to improve her performance in coursework and in exams.

Note: If you want to try out this method, you will find further information in Appendix 14, page 66.

Karen's background

Karen was a first-year student in a school of health studies, attached to a northern university. She had never been very successful in her schooldays, but she had decided to train as a nurse after working as, among other things, a care assistant and enjoying it very much. To meet the entry requirements for her nursing course she had completed a course and gained a certificate from a college of further education.

This had been quite a challenge. As a result, she came to feel that some of the academic sections of her university course might be too difficult for her. She had problems with her studies during her first year and was uncertain that she could go on. However, she was referred for screening and a diagnostic assessment for dyslexia and she was identified as having dyslexia. Her report recommended that Karen should work with a specialist tutor, as follows.

Step 1: Planning and organizing written work

It was agreed between Karen and her tutor that she would begin by developing ways of planning her written work. Such plans were definitely helpful in improving Karen's ability to focus on understanding a given question. They also helped her to develop selective reading and note-taking techniques. However, such plans were based on the written word and so depended almost entirely on Karen's weak visual memory.

Step 2: Revision and examination techniques

Karen's past experiences of study had severely damaged her confidence in her ability to pass exams. However, the continuation on her course depended on this, so she was determined to find ways of improving her performance. She felt this was so important that she opted to concentrate on such techniques as a priority. It was at this point that her tutor suggested that building on Karen's reliable auditory memory might offer her a way forward.

Step 3: Coping with short questions in exams

Karen's first exam paper would consist of 30 short questions to be answered in one hour.

Revision method

1   Karen obtained past papers and answered the questions in writing.

2   She checked her answers for accuracy from notes and textbooks.

3   She began to practise speaking her answers into a tape recorder.

Problems

In early trials of this method, Karen felt very self-conscious and was unsure that the recommended method would produce the required results. However, she decided to continue and used a tape recorder for her first exam.

Results

•   In practice sessions, Karen quickly reached a stage where she could answer questions quickly, e.g.15 answers on tape in 19 minutes.

•   In the examination, she was easily able to answer 30 questions in 53 minutes.

•   Karen gained 64% and this was by far her highest score ever.

•   Karen decided to seek permission to revise and present all her examination papers in this way.

What happened next?

Staff in the School of Health Studies were willing to accept a recommendation that this alternative method of assessment should be used by Karen throughout her course.

However, it was also agreed that further work would need to be done in relation to answering different types of questions, as follows.

Answering essay-type exam questions

Karen would focus on clarifying the main points of her answer in her opening words. In effect, this would provide her with a basic plan, which she would be able to recall, via her short-term auditory memory.

As her revision practice developed further, Karen introduced the idea of creating her own graphic images to represent the key issues she needed to cover. These were sketched out in rough as part of the initial preparations to answer a given question.

Instructions for transcription

At an early stage, it was agreed that Karen would develop a standardized method of making clear her intentions to the person transcribing the tapes. This included clear statements about the following:

- candidate's name and number
- start and end time for questions
- deletions and substitutions
- corrections of minor errors, such as dates and names.

Conclusion

Karen was able to gain greatly improved marks in her examinations. For example, for one of her papers in her final exams she was awarded 67%.

In addition, she decided to make as much use as possible of tapes to plan, organize and draft an assignment before putting it into writing. This was carried out with the approval of academic staff, who were willing to comment constructively on her methods and her work, especially in the first year of her course.

Karen's confidence in her own abilities to meet the demands of her course began to grow. Her marks for coursework and in exams improved; no extensions or resits were required. Finally, Karen gained the qualification she needed to enter her chosen profession. She intends to continue to use a tape recorder wherever possible in her work on the wards.

Using a tape recorder for examinations

Procedures

1   Check whether there is a recommendation/suggestion concerning your short-term auditory memory in your assessment report for dyslexia. There may also be recommendations/suggestions about ways of achieving improvement.

Note: This is the basis on which this option is likely to be open to you.

2   Be prepared to commit yourself to the time and effort necessary to ensure that this method works for you. It is likely to involve using a tape recorder regularly in a range of situations so that it becomes a natural way of working.

3   Discuss your options with your lecturers, personal tutor, and Disability Office staff.

4   Ensure that the decision to use a tape recorder in examinations is passed on to relevant people, e.g. appropriate staff in school, faculty, department, Disability Office, Examinations Office at least six weeks before the examination takes place.

Things to consider carefully

Clear communication

Throughout, it is important to remember that one of your main objectives is to dictate answers into a tape recorder, which an audio typist can transcribe easily and accurately, so that your work can be assessed by internal and external examiners. Remember that you can speak much faster than you can write, but your answers must be clearly spoken and structured as clearly as possible.

Your feelings

You also need to allow for the possibility that you might feel uncomfortable when you begin to use the technique of speaking into a machine to answer questions. However, experience indicates that such feelings soon fade as students adapt and realize the personal benefits that the new technique can bring.

The examination

Remember that you will be alone in an examination room with appropriate equipment and an invigilator. Also, no extra time will be allowed, because speech is produced much faster than the written word. This means that you should pace yourself to use some time for silently thinking out your answers, possibly accompanied by brief notes or a list of key words/topics to help you to remember to cover all the questions as fully as possible.

Transferable skills

It is also worth bearing in mind that the skill of using a tape recorder can be used in many different ways. For example, as a student and also as an employee, you can record notes, make lists of things to be done, plan, draft and dictate reports, case studies, portfolios, letters and other documents.

Methods for revision

Stage 1

- Acquire examples of past papers.

- Use the instructions on examination papers to identify how much time to allow to answer each question.

- Choose a question on which to practise.

- Revise the information needed to answer it.

- At this early stage, allow yourself only 15 minutes of thinking and speaking time.

Stage 2

- Make sure your tape recorder will take tapes lasting for 3 hours (maximum examination time).

- Make sure you have a microphone suited to your needs, e.g. lapel, freestanding, conference microphone.

- Set up and test equipment and time your first practice session, e.g. 15 minutes only.

- Start by practising speaking in a clear and logical way.

- Avoid repeating words.

- If in doubt or lost for words, be silent, rather than using fillers such as 'I can't remember that bit' or 'Er'.

- Playback and listen critically to your own words.

- Practise so that you improve on your own performance.

Stage 3

Build in instructions to typist, for example:

• Provide all information in spoken words required to be written on the front cover of the answer paper.

• Say the number of the question clearly and, if you like, read the question out loud.

• Say 'Answer' before you start to dictate.

• Say 'End of question' and pause before moving on.

Extend practice until you can answer in spoken words the whole of a paper as in a mock exam.

Tim and his memory

Are you good at remembering what you see?

Many students who have dyslexia find that they can remember what they see better than what they hear. (The assessment report provided by your psychologist should normally make it clear if your short-term visual memory is more reliable than you short-term auditory memory.)

Read about Tim to see how he found ways to improve his performance in coursework and exams.

Tim's background

Tim went on from school to complete a course in art and design at his local college of further education. He then gained a place at university to study for a degree in electronic imaging and media studies.

Staff in the Disability Office at his university arranged for him to have an update of his diagnostic assessment for dyslexia. This recommended that he should purchase a PC, with appropriate software, which could be funded by a DSA.

Tim enjoyed the first semester of his course, but soon began to feel that he was losing his way in a sea of paper. He was collecting larger and larger quantities of notes from books, and even more from lectures and seminars.

He knew that these notes were very important because he had always had problems retaining and recalling what people said to him. He was also given many handouts relevant to his studies and to his exams. In addition, he was expected to produce a substantial amount of written work each semester.

Feeling desperate, he made an appointment for a confidential interview with the Disability Officer. Tim outlined his difficulties and asked for advice on what to do. After some discussion, it was agreed that the best way forward was for Tim to build on his visual strengths and abilities.

It was agreed that Tim would begin by using colour and some graphics to help him to sort out his paperwork.

Step 1: Organizing notes and handouts

- Tim chose a different coloured file for each module.

- He labelled it clearly, adding, wherever possible, a picture, cartoon or symbol as an aid to quick recognition.

- He used different coloured paper, e.g. pale blue for notes from lectures, yellow for notes from books and articles.

- He used different coloured stickers (available from stationers) to help him identify and group his handouts.

- He also began to use different coloured highlighters to identify important points in handouts and in his own notes.

Step 2: Organizing time and meeting deadlines

Tim wanted to make sure that his work was completed and handed in on time, so he was advised to create a computer file for his timetable. This was then expanded to include deadlines for the completion of written work and for exams, alongside his programme of lectures and seminars.

Step 3: Planning written work

Tim was encouraged to use methods relying on lines and shapes when planning an essay or report. He used mind maps, spider diagrams, graphics, sketches, flowcharts and bar charts to help him create visual sequences on which he could base his written work. This material was then filed with his completed assigment for revision purposes.

Step 4: On screen: using colours and shapes

Tim learned that he could easily vary the background colour of his computer screen. He found that he felt most comfortable with a yellow background and black print. In early drafts, he could also use double spacing and different sized fonts (the shape and size of individual letters). In addition, Tim found it helpful to print out copies of this preparatory work in the colours and fonts he liked best. However, he was always careful to revert to the required standard font when he printed out his final draft.

Conclusion

Tim continued to develop his own methods of building on his visual strengths throughout his course. In common with many students with dyslexia, he found that using coloured paper instead of white was a great help when writing. He also began to feel that placing a coloured transparency (soft yellow in his case) over a printed page made it easier for him to read. (See below for more information on this.)

In the final year of his course, Tim was given the opportunity to write a dissertation on the effects of colour on the perception of people with dyslexia. He presented this work in an innovative way, using graphics, interviews, video and samples of timed tests to support the written text. For this, he was awarded the departmental final year prize.

Colour sensitivity and dyslexia

Does this happen to you?

Many people with dyslexia find the act of reading difficult for a number of reasons:

- eye strain because of the glare of print on paper

- blurring of vision

- apparent movement of print.

What might help

1   Experiment with pastel colours of A4 cartridge paper to see if you can reduce discomfort when writing by hand or reading printouts of your own work.

2   Try out soft shades of peach, yellow, green or blue. These colours and others too are available from stationers.

3   Change the background colour of your computer screen until you find one that is pleasant to use.

4   Experiment with coloured transparencies over the printed page. You may find that print ceases to 'jump about' and blurring is reduced.

Tinted lenses

Some find that their problems can be reduced by the prescription of tinted lenses for reading glasses. A number of opticians offer a special eye test for this purpose. Contact your LEA to see if it would be possible to claim the costs of such an eye test via the DSA.

Further information is available from: The Irlen Institute, Lansdowne College, 43 Harrington Gardens, London SW7 4JU.

For transparencies and information about special eye tests contact: Cerium Ltd (tel: 01580 765211).

References and resources

For obvious reasons, entries are restricted. The resources mentioned are good examples of their type. All items have been tried and tested by students.

Computer programs
The British Dyslexia Association (98 London Road, Reading RG1 5AU; tel: 01734 668 271) regularly reviews study support and maths software. Ask for the latest leaflet.

The following may also be of help:
1   **ThinkSheet** (a 3-D planning tool that enables you to organize your brainstorming. Ideas can be added as you think of them and then linked to mind maps). Available from Fisher-Marriot, 58 Victoria Road, Woodbridge, Suffolk IP12 1EL; tel: 01394 387 050.

2   **Wordshark** (a structured, cumulative and progressive reading/spelling program. Its graphics may not appeal to older learners but it is very thorough. No other program matches its close links with Hornsby and Shear's Alpha to Omega.). Available from White Space Ltd, 41 Mall Road, London W6 9DG; tel/fax: 020 8748 5927.

3   **Mathsblaster.** Again, the graphics may be offputting but this is a good, structured maths program. Available from ABLAC/Computec Ltd, South Devon House, Newton Abbot, Devon TQ12 2BP; tel: 0626 332233.

4   **Texthelp** (an integrated package for dyslexic and speech/vision and mobility impaired students. It has speech feedback, automatic word endings, spell checker, specialist dictionaries, etc.). Available from Lorien Systems Ltd, 25 Randalstown Road, Antrim BT41 4LJ; tel: 01849 428 105.

5   **Fairley House Micro-type** (a touch-typing program and companion practice sheets). Available from IEC, 77 Orton Lane, Wombourne, Staffs WV5 9AP; tel: 0902 722 012.

6   On-line help with spelling/meaning/expression:
    • www.facstaff.bucknell.edu/rbeard/diction.html
    • www.westegg.co/cliche/
    • www.thesaurus.com/

Helpful books

1   *Dyslexia, a Guide for Dyslexic Adults.* British Dyslexia Assocation, 98 London Road, Reading RG1 5AU; tel: 0118 966 2677.

2   Buzan T (1990) *Use your Head.* BBC Books, London. Explains how to make the best use of your brain, and teaches mind-mapping and recall skills.

3   Heaton P and Mitchell G (1999) *Learning to Learn.* Dyslexia Unit, 169, Midland Road, Royston, Barnsley S71 4BZ; tel: 01226 726 459. A study skills course and exercises for post-16 students.

4   Henderson A (1989) *Maths and Dyslexia.* St David's College, Conway Road, Llandudno, North Wales LL30 1RD (written enquiries only). Describes ways of helping dyslexics develop number skills.

5   Hornsby and Shear (1993) *Alpha to Omega.* Heinemann, Oxford. A structured/cumulative and progressive reading

and spelling programme – well recommended by many dyslexics.

6   Leader W (1984) *How to Pass Exams.* Macdonald and Evans, London. A small handbook on revision and exam techniques.

7   Stirling E (1985) *Help for the Dyslexic Adolescent.* St David's College, Conway Road, Llandudno, North Wales LL30 1RD (written enquiries only). Practical tips from an experienced specialist teacher.

Useful addresses

1   **Adult Dyslexia Organisation,** 336 Brixton Road, London SW9 7AA; tel: 020 7737 7646. The organization links adult dyslexics across Britain. It gives advice on education, careers, funding and resources.

2   **British Dyslexia Association,** 98 London Road, Reading RG1 5AU; tel: 0118 966 2677. The 'mother' charity – a first port of call for many dyslexics. Deals with any and every aspect of dyslexia.

3   **Dyslexia Institute,** 133 Gresham Road, Staines; tel: 01784 463 852. The Institute has outposts across the country. It offers advice, assessment and teaching.

4   Local dyslexia associations and support groups are generally listed in free press, local libraries and telephone directories.

5   **Graduate Support Scheme for Graduates and Undergraduates with a Disability** (often known as WORKABLE). Contacts are as follows:

- London, tel: 020 7222 1803
- Reading, Thames Valley and Oxford, tel: 0118 961 9308
- Manchester, tel: 0161 272 7800
- Cambridge, tel: 01223 363 271(ext. 2316).

WORKABLE helps graduates and undergraduates with CV writing, application forms and arranging work placements.

6   **Peter Honey Publications**, 10 Linden Avenue, Maidenhead, Berkshire SL6 6HB; tel 01628 633 946; web site: www.peterhoney.co.uk Publishes literature/tests on learning style.

7   **SKILL: National Bureau for Students with Disabilities**, Chapter House, 18-20 Crucifix Lane, London SE1 3JW; tel: 0800 068 2422 (afternoons only, Monday to Friday); e-mail SkillNatBurDis@compuserve.com

8   **Department of Education and Employment**, Student Support, Division 1, Room 215, Mowden Hall, Staindrop Road, Darlington DL3 9BG; tel: 01325 392822.

9   **National Federation of Access** supplies information on the assessment of support needs in locations across the country; tel: 01752 232279.

Index